Gallery Books
Editor: Peter Fallon

GHOSTS

Thomas Kilroy

GHOSTS

after Ibsen

Gallery Books

Ghosts
is first published
simultaneously in paperback
and in a clothbound edition
in April 2002.

The Gallery Press
Loughcrew
Oldcastle
County Meath
Ireland

© Thomas Kilroy 2002

ISBN 1 85235 310 4 (*paperback*)
    1 85235 311 2 (*clothbound*)

A CIP catalogue record for this book
is available from the British Library.

   The Gallery Press acknowledges the financial assistance of
An Chomhairle Ealaíon / The Arts Council, Ireland, and the Arts
Council of Northern Ireland.

for Phyllis Ryan and the late Siobhán McKenna
who first asked me to make this adaptation

Characters

MRS HELEN AYLWARD, *a widow*
OLIVER, *her son, late twenties*
FR MANNING, *a Roman Catholic priest*
JACKO ENGLISH, *an odd-job man, late sixties*
REGINA, *his putative daughter, mid-twenties*

The play is set in the mid-1980s in a house on the outskirts of a small Irish provincial town.

Thomas Kilroy's *Ghosts* was first produced by the Abbey Theatre, in association with Gemini Productions, at the Peacock Theatre, Dublin, on Thursday, 5 October 1989, as part of the Dublin Theatre Festival, with the following cast:

MRS AYLWARD	Doreen Hepburn
OLIVER	Conor Mullen
FR MANNING	David Kelly
JACKO ENGLISH	Kevin Flood
REGINA	Noelle Brown

Director	Michael Scott
Set Designer	Geraldine O'Malley
Lighting	Leslie Scott

The play was revised by Thomas Kilroy and toured by the Brown Penny Theatre Company in 2002.

'To marry for external reasons, even when these are religious or moral reasons, brings a nemesis down upon the children.'

—Henrik Ibsen

ACT ONE

The Aylward family's living-room in a large, handsome house on the edge of an Irish provincial town.

Heavy furniture and wall-paper, stolid, moneyed taste. Although there are three doors and a window, the effect is claustrophobic. The one exception and the source of light is the French window, centre, which leads beyond to a quite spectacular conservatory. This eventually opens out as another acting area.

REGINA *is tidying up when a wet* FR MANNING, *carrying a briefcase and shaking his umbrella, comes in behind her.*

REGINA Father! You got the train OK!

FR MANNING Isn't it dreadful, the weather!

REGINA Here — give me yer coat. Can I take the brief-case?

FR MANNING No — no, that's one bag I can't let out of my sight, Regina. That bag has treasure in it, so it has. And how're you these days?

REGINA I'm OK.

FR MANNING Plenty to do? (REGINA *shrugs and he looks at her for a moment*) And Mrs Aylward?

REGINA She's above with Oliver — I mean Mr Aylward. (*Rush*) He won't go near a doctor — Mrs Aylward says he's only run down but I think he looks terrible. I know I shouldn't be saying that, now, so I shouldn't.

FR MANNING When did he get back from Paris?

REGINA He sweats. God, how he sweats. The sheets are wringing wet every morning when I touch them.

FR MANNING Maybe the boy has a chill — travel and that.

REGINA Father, could you talk to him? About going to a doctor?

11

FR MANNING   Oh, now I couldn't do that, child. Of course I was concerned when I heard about his illness. Very concerned, very concerned indeed, who wouldn't be? (*Looking off*) But you can't come between a mother and a son, Regina.

REGINA   (*Sullenly*) 'Course.

FR MANNING   (*Looking back at her*) You've changed, Regina.

REGINA   What way, changed?

FR MANNING   Since I saw you last. Appearance, maybe.

REGINA   Mr Aylward says I've filled out!

FR MANNING   Are you trying to tease me, Regina?

REGINA   'Deed I'm not.

FR MANNING   I never know where I am these days with young people — (*A pause*) Is your father around?

REGINA   He's down finishing the new buildings with the other men.

FR MANNING   They'd better be finished for tomorrow's opening ceremony. You know I was talking to him, Jacko, only the other day, Regina. About yourself.

REGINA   Don't want to hear it.

FR MANNING   He *is* your father —

REGINA   He's a sentimental slob and a cripple into the bargain! (*He lets her suffer for this remark*) I know I shouldn't talk like that. 'Bout anywan. But if there's wan thing I can't stand 'tis pretending this and pretending that!

FR MANNING   Ah, you have to be patient with him, Regina. Sure, poor Jacko's not too strong a character. Though he means well. I'll say that much for him.

REGINA   He's an alcoholic and I'm not going to live with him and that's that. Anyway, I'm needed here.

FR MANNING   It might be your bounden duty to go live with him, child.

REGINA   (*Scorn*) Duty!

FR MANNING   Yes, duty. I know it's not a fashionable word nowadays. Besides his whole future might depend upon it. Someone by his side. He may not be able to manage otherwise.

REGINA   I'm not going to run a B & B for him, no way!
That's what he wants, y'know.

FR MANNING   A B & B! That's the first I've heard of this.

REGINA   A B & B! Whoever heard the likes? He's going to
talk to you about it. If I'm going to be a skivvy,
I'd prefer to be a skivvy for someone else.

FR MANNING   (*Dismissing the idea*) Maybe we should talk it
over with Mrs Aylward.

REGINA   Someone like me doesn't have any choices.

FR MANNING   That's not true, now.

REGINA   Maybe I'll put an ad in the paper. Respectable
maid. Clean. Good worker. Anxious to meet fat
farmer. Send photo.

FR MANNING   You shouldn't make jokes about such things,
Regina.

REGINA   What about young Mr Aylward?

FR MANNING   What about him?

REGINA   (*Sullenly*) Nuthing.

FR MANNING   What about him? (*No answer. He doesn't like this*)
I see. Maybe you'd better go call Mrs Aylward,
so.

REGINA   (*Brazenly*) Yes, Father. Certainly, Father. 'Course,
Father.

> FR MANNING *lets out a long sigh. He examines*
> *the titles of books on the table and shakes his head*
> *at what he sees.* MRS AYLWARD *enters with*
> REGINA *who stands, briefly, in the doorway.*

MRS AYLWARD   Well! You got here at last. It's been a while.

FR MANNING   This is one occasion I was determined to be
here.

MRS AYLWARD   (*Holding him by the arms*) Here — let me look at
you! It means everything to me that you could
make it. (*An intimate moment: she looks at* REGINA)
That will be all for the moment, Regina. (REGINA
exits. Exasperation) Oh, Regina! (*They look at one
another*) Where're your bags?

FR MANNING   I booked in to the Station Hotel.

MRS AYLWARD	I see.
FR MANNING	It's better that way.
MRS AYLWARD	The same as ever. On the dot. Everything in place. You know you should have been an accountant or something.
FR MANNING	Well, I try to take care of my responsibilities if that's what you mean.
MRS AYLWARD	I'm sorry. I didn't mean to mock you. I would have liked you to stay in the house. Just this once.
FR MANNING	It wouldn't be right, Helen, and you know that as well as myself.
MRS AYLWARD	Do you never, ever, regret the past? Don't answer that. Forget it.
FR MANNING	Something's troubling you? Do you want to talk about it?
MRS AYLWARD	It's only tomorrow. The opening of that building. Remembering Martin's death. And now Oliver home. All the past flooding in again. Don't you remember?
FR MANNING	Isn't it great he's back home again, Oliver?
MRS AYLWARD	He's going to — stay.
FR MANNING	And doesn't that please you? It's wonderful news.
MRS AYLWARD	(*High, forced tone, quickly*) Oh, he's great. I mean he's in great form — 'course he's changed a bit — who hasn't? He wants to show his work, maybe a local exhibition. It's no wonder he's exhausted. All that effort. (*She breaks in distress*)
FR MANNING	What is it, dear?
MRS AYLWARD	(*New tears*) There's something — wrong with him. I don't know. He's so — gaunt, so — edgy. And people no longer recognize him. Do you know that? They say: this couldn't be Oliver. (*Hurriedly*) Let me see those papers now.
FR MANNING	Please let me help you.
MRS AYLWARD	Does it ever occur to you that your help may do more harm than good?
FR MANNING	My goodness, what a thing to say!

*He opens the briefcase beside the books, picks up
one of them and turns it over.*

MRS AYLWARD Think about it. (*Pause*) Well, 'tis true. You've
always been the same. Going around trying to
sort out other people's lives for them.

FR MANNING I do help people.

MRS AYLWARD I know you help people. That's not the point.
Are you sure going around doing good, as you
see it, doesn't sometimes cause great suffering?

FR MANNING (*Pause*) That's a strange notion and no mistake.
(*Pause*) I'm not sure about everything. I don't
pretend to know — everything. But one thing I
am sure of is the teaching of our Lord and
Saviour Jesus Christ.

MRS AYLWARD I think we have to grope towards our morality
every hour of every day of our lives. (*Pause*) Oh,
I know you mean well. Here. We'll look at those
papers.

FR MANNING Here they are. Is everything finished with the
builders?

MRS AYLWARD Jacko English and some of the men are just
tidying up down there.

He points to one of the books on the table.

FR MANNING And is this what you're reading now? (*She nods*)
There's no doubt but this country is upside down.

MRS AYLWARD And about time, too. These are the nineteen
eighties, for heaven's sakes. Of course things
have changed.

FR MANNING I'm not going to argue with you.

MRS AYLWARD What you really mean is that you're above
argument. (*He laughs silently*) What's so funny?

FR MANNING Round and round we go in circles again. Don't
you remember? How we used to argue in the past?

MRS AYLWARD You're a very stubborn man, you know that?

FR MANNING Oh, I can move all right. When it's right to move.

MRS AYLWARD I seem to progress at a snail's pace. One step

forward, two steps back.

FR MANNING And you call this (*towards the books*) progress? Attacks on the home, the family, on womanhood itself? I grant you this. We're always the same in this country. Picking up the last year's fashion when it's being dropped everywhere else.

MRS AYLWARD That's nonsense.

FR MANNING No, it is not nonsense. Everywhere people are turning back to religion. Just when we're rapidly getting rid of our traditional values in Ireland, everyone else is turning back to them again. And what about tomorrow? The opening and blessing of the new building?

MRS AYLWARD What about it?

FR MANNING Here you are. Giving all this money from your husband's legacy to a badly needed charity for abused women. And at the same time preaching licence.

MRS AYLWARD I'm not preaching anything. I'm just trying to come to terms with things. The past. You see I'm trying to make up for lost time. Don't you understand? (*Pause*) Anyway, no one's going to tell me what books to read at my age.

FR MANNING My dear, you have to rely on the guidance of others. I do. We all do. That's what life is all about.

MRS AYLWARD Not for me. Not anymore.

FR MANNING I see. Well, I've all the papers ready here for you. I can tell the bishop took some persuading. I mean, it'd be different if the bequest had been made directly to the Church for disposing as charity. Still I said that, perhaps, it was about time that the Church started to rely upon private foundations, people of good standing, of course, to help in carrying on the good work. I believe more and more charitable institutions will be run like this in the future by private groups.

MRS AYLWARD So this is it at last!

FR MANNING   This is it. The Aylward Centre for Women and
              Children. Are you sure about the name? Is it not
              a bit secular?

MRS AYLWARD   (*Urgently*) Yes — yes. It must have Martin's
              name on it! It must!

FR MANNING   Here are the bank documents. The interest will
              all go towards the day-to-day running of the
              place and —

MRS AYLWARD   You keep all that in your hands. I don't want to
              touch it!

FR MANNING   But what about Oliver?

MRS AYLWARD   Oliver? What has Oliver got to do with it? Oliver
              has nothing to do with any of this!

FR MANNING   I'm only a caretaker, you know. Properly speak-
              ing, Oliver should be in charge.

MRS AYLWARD   (*Considerable force*) Oliver must be kept away
              from all this! (*Long pause*) I will take care of Oliver.

FR MANNING   Yes. Well, there's a couple of other things. One, I
              propose we double the valuation which you
              have here. For insurance purposes, of course.
              We have an extremely valuable property here,
              you know. On a prime site.

MRS AYLWARD   And two? What's the second?

FR MANNING   Well — discretion.

MRS AYLWARD   Discretion?

FR MANNING   Certainly. The need to be discreet. What I mean
              is, it's very important that my name should not
              be connected, at all. You get my point?

MRS AYLWARD   You mean I shouldn't gossip.

FR MANNING   Oh, more than that, more than that, now.

MRS AYLWARD   But you're not even a beneficiary.

FR MANNING   I know — I know — I know. In the event of the
              project coming to an end it all reverts to the
              Church. I know that. It's just — my name.

MRS AYLWARD   Oh — really!

FR MANNING   It's these journalists. You know what they tried
              to do to me in the past over money. They would
              crucify me if they had half a chance.

MRS AYLWARD   We won't allow your name in the papers.

FR MANNING	Don't make light of it, please.
MRS AYLWARD	Can we get on to the other details?
FR MANNING	Elements in the media in this country are out to destroy the Church. I know them. You know them.
MRS AYLWARD	You've said enough. My lips are sealed. Just stay out of the photos!
FR MANNING	It really is an awful, a distressing thing, money. I dislike the whole question of money, you know.
MRS AYLWARD	Funny you should mention insurance. You know, we almost had a fire down there the other day. In the new building.
FR MANNING	Had a what?
MRS AYLWARD	Yes. Fire.
FR MANNING	Not serious, I hope.
MRS AYLWARD	No. Just shavings under the carpenter's bench.
FR MANNING	You mean Jacko English?
MRS AYLWARD	The very man. The butt of a cigarette.
FR MANNING	Oh, the ruffian — the ruffian. Still, we have to have an understanding of the weaknesses of others. He's doing his best to turn over a new leaf.
MRS AYLWARD	Who?
FR MANNING	Jacko.
MRS AYLWARD	And who told you that?
FR MANNING	He did. Himself.
MRS AYLWARD	Well, if you believe that you'll believe anything.
FR MANNING	Come on, now. He's not that bad. A bit rough at the edges. If he has a drink too much itself it's because of that constant pain. That leg of his. Dreadful.
MRS AYLWARD	You're unbelievable. You really are.
FR MANNING	I believe we must always try to think the best of people. And when we do it's surprising how people — Anyway, Jacko is very grateful for the job you gave him here. So that he can be near Regina.
MRS AYLWARD	Not that he bothers much about her.
FR MANNING	Oh, but he does, he does. By the way, the last time I saw him he asked — what do you think?

	He wants to take Regina back to live with him. He apparently wants to go into business.
MRS AYLWARD	(*Jump*) Regina! Absolutely out of the question. The very thought of it. Besides, Regina is going to have a job here. In the new home for women and children. She'll have plenty to do down there, plenty.
FR MANNING	I see. The way you go on, well, 'tis almost as if you're afraid of him.
MRS AYLWARD	Maybe I am.
FR MANNING	Jacko? Is it Jacko? Impossible, surely. Afraid of Jacko!

Door bangs shut off. Pause.

| MRS AYLWARD | That's Oliver. I don't want him — Not another word, now, about this business with Regina. |

OLIVER *enters. He is carrying a long-stemmed pipe. Pale and gaunt, he stands before them.*

OLIVER	Sorry. Thought you were on your own. Oh, it's Fr Manning. Hi ya, Father.
FR MANNING	Good Heavens! He is just like him —
MRS AYLWARD	(*A rush*) Now, Fr Manning, doesn't he look well? Doesn't he, though? I keep telling him he looks fine. You do, Oliver. You do.
OLIVER	Mother! Please! Cut it out, would you.
MRS AYLWARD	A little run down, maybe. That's all. Otherwise you look great. Doesn't he, Father? Look great?
FR MANNING	It's the face. So like his Dad. That's what stopped me in my tracks.
OLIVER	Last time we met you said I was damned.
MRS AYLWARD	That's unnecessary, Oliver.
FR MANNING	Oh, I don't mind a bit. I like a sense of humour in young fellows. I do. I do. I do.
OLIVER	I'm back from the corruption of the continent.
FR MANNING	Oh, now —
OLIVER	But that's what you said to me, wasn't it?

'Beware the corruption of the continent, young man.'

MRS AYLWARD Fr Manning was thinking of your well-being.

OLIVER Sure.

FR MANNING Well, it's true, you know. I mean it's a long, long fight against secular humanism. But the tide will turn. Of that I'm certain.

MRS AYLWARD Oliver is good-living, Father.

OLIVER Oh, for God's sake!

MRS AYLWARD You just have to look at him to know.

OLIVER If this continues I'm leaving!

An awkward pause.

FR MANNING I've seen some of your reviews, you know.

OLIVER You what?

FR MANNING Reviews. Of your work. Painting. Some time ago it was. High praise. Great promise.

OLIVER I'm not painting now —

MRS AYLWARD (*In a rush*) Rest is very important for the artist.

FR MANNING Certainly. Inspiration. Time to think things out. All the great artists were like that.

OLIVER That's a laugh. Sorry. I didn't mean to be — What time is lunch at?

MRS AYLWARD It'll be soon, dear. (*Almost desperate*) What an appetite! He has a wonderful appetite, Father. Thanks be to God.

FR MANNING And I see he smokes.

OLIVER (*Ironical*) He sure does.

MRS AYLWARD (*Trying to convince herself*) It's a great sign. A good appetite.

OLIVER (*To the pipe*) This is my father's old pot of dreams.

MRS AYLWARD (*Clenched teeth*) Dear, I wish you wouldn't speak like that. (*She explodes so that both men are taken aback*) And I wish you wouldn't bring that thing downstairs!

OLIVER Sorry.

FR MANNING But, of course. I see it now. It's the pipe!

MRS AYLWARD I told you, Oliver, not to bring that dirty thing down here!

FR MANNING Oliver. When he stood there. With the — in his hand. I said: Aylward. I said to myself: the living image of his dead father. Martin Aylward all over again.

OLIVER (*Not amused*) Oho, that's a good one! Ho-ho-ho.

MRS AYLWARD Nonsense. Oliver always took after me.

OLIVER Good old Da!

FR MANNING It's the mouth, maybe. I mean around the lips, the living spit of Martin Aylward. The pipe. That look.

MRS AYLWARD (*Strained*) He's not in the least bit like his father. There is something quite refined in Oliver's face which Martin never had.

OLIVER Oh, my God.

FR MANNING Indeed you're right. A spiritual quality. Many saintly priests have that quality too.

MRS AYLWARD (*Explosively*) Oliver! Put that pipe away at once!

Both men are again taken aback by her vehemence.

OLIVER It brings back my childhood. The happy memories.

MRS AYLWARD Oliver!

OLIVER Sitting on my Daddy's knee. The two of us high as kites. 'Here, my boy. Have a drag.' And he puffed. And I puffed. And we went down the Sewanee river together.

FR MANNING What's that? What's that?

MRS AYLWARD It's only a crude joke, Father. Pay no heed to him. Please, Oliver.

OLIVER Then Mother came in. Grabbed me up. She was crying. I couldn't understand why she was crying. While he was laughing. (*Deadpan*) Ho-ho. (*Quietly*) He was quite something, my Daddy.

FR MANNING As a young man he might have been a bit irresponsible. Full of the joy of life.

MRS AYLWARD Could we change the subject? Please.

OLIVER Actually, I believe that. The joy of life. He would

have gobbled up life if it hadn't gobbled him up, first.

FR MANNING A great man. Highly respected. Did more for his country in his short life than many who lived to old age.

OLIVER I was thinking of the private man. Not the public one.

MRS AYLWARD (*Again, highly stressed*) That man is dead and buried!

She turns away from the two men.

FR MANNING Well, now! You're here for the opening of the women's shelter, isn't it great? Your father's bequest!

MRS AYLWARD (*Struggling to be bright*) And he's going to stay, Father! I'm going to hold on to him —

OLIVER If this bloody weather doesn't kill me. That's a joke. Don't mind me, I'm just full of crap.

MRS AYLWARD — at least until the spring.

OLIVER You know, I think I must have been emotionally retarded growing up. It's as if I never had an adolescence.

FR MANNING Well, that's more or less what I meant — when you first went away, I mean. My advice to you. I had your spiritual welfare in mind, you see.

MRS AYLWARD I think it's terribly important that young people get away. Especially nowadays. Especially from this country.

FR MANNING What on earth do you mean?

OLIVER Yes. Nurture. I mean, if it's incomplete, nurture, in the child, there is no adulthood. Is there?

FR MANNING Nurture. Exactly. Family life. Christian, family life. Now, Mrs Aylward, take the case of Oliver, there! (*She gestures*) No, no, no, no. I'm going to speak in front of the boy. I am. I am. Adrift. Drifting about for years without a proper family environment —

MRS AYLWARD I resent that remark, Fr Manning!

FR MANNING Now I know you've done your level best in very difficult circumstances —

MRS AYLWARD The boy, as you put it, is nearly twenty-seven years of age.

OLIVER Actually, I think so called family works for very few people. (*Pause*) There is more evil propagated inside family life than in any other human organization that I know of.

Long pause.

FR MANNING That's an awful thing to say! Awful!

MRS AYLWARD But Oliver! You spoke so warmly about coming home.

OLIVER What I meant was — I meant, simply, love.

FR MANNING Well, now. I take that point. I think I understand what Oliver is saying. Yes, yes, I do. But all this business of freedom and so on and so on — it's all old hat now, don't you know. The world has changed. Old values are returning.

OLIVER Yes, the world has changed.

FR MANNING Young people of my acquaintance now are flocking back to religion. Daily Mass-goers. Communicants. Illicit unions are being regularized. Order is being restored.

OLIVER You use such quaint language, Father.

FR MANNING My dear boy, I'm too old to be baited.

OLIVER Illicit unions!

FR MANNING You know perfectly well what I mean.

OLIVER Do you mean man and woman? Or man and man? Or woman and woman? Or some other combination?

FR MANNING You can't shock me, Oliver.

OLIVER Oh, I'm not trying to shock you, Father. I'm simply trying to establish what we're talking about. Not easy, mind you.

The pace of delivery suddenly picks up.

FR MANNING   I'm certainly not talking about abnormality —

OLIVER   — thought we were talking about love —

FR MANNING   — love! Indeed!

OLIVER   You don't think homosexuals can express love?

FR MANNING   — but you do?

OLIVER   — 'course —

FR MANNING   And children?

OLIVER   What about them?

FR MANNING   — exposed to this kind of thing?

OLIVER   (*Slowing down again*) I've seen children exposed, as you put it, to this kind of thing. Growing up perfectly normal, as you put it. But without fear, without disgust, without guilt.

MRS AYLWARD   Father — how would you counsel people attracted in this way?

FR MANNING   Celibacy.

OLIVER   That won't get you very far, I'm afraid.

MRS AYLWARD   Afraid not.

FR MANNING   I tell you the laws are coming back. In country after country, the laws are coming back to deal with this corruption. Mrs Aylward! I must say this. I have to say this to you. Why do you sit there, silent, while your own son surrenders himself in this way to gross immorality?

OLIVER   Let me tell you something, Father —

MRS AYLWARD   No, Oliver, don't —

FR MANNING   Despicable talk!

OLIVER   I'll give you despicable talk, immorality, the lot, the real thing, Father. And people you know well.

FR MANNING   What people?

OLIVER   The ones who wine and dine the clergy, that's who. Our great businessmen and politicians. By God, when it all comes out, that'll be the day! All the dirty linen of the Faith of our Fathers!

FR MANNING   What exactly are you talking about?

OLIVER   Let me tell you what happens to these boyos when they get away from their wives and children and their precious Church. One day six of them arrived on my doorstep. Grinning,

	red-faced guys, do you want their names? No, 'course not. Over for a high level conference, no less. Got my address from Mother here. Looking for a bit of action, they said. And given my arty life could I set them up. Then they listed their needs. Every kink in the book. I just listened.
MRS AYLWARD	Oliver!
OLIVER	I'll spare you the details, Mother. I threw them out. That look on their faces. Not fear, not shame, oh, no. The look of power that if I ever dared to open my mouth they would —
MRS AYLWARD	I think you should lie down, Oliver.
OLIVER	Didn't mean to upset you, Mother, not like that.

REGINA *appears with a tray in the conservatory.*
FR MANNING *watches what follows, very carefully.*

REGINA	Will you have lunch in here, Missus?
MRS AYLWARD	What? Oh — yes —
REGINA	(*Coquettishly*) Would you like the red wine or the white wine, Mr Aylward?
OLIVER	(*Brightening*) Oh, sure, I'd like the two of them, Miss English!
MRS AYLWARD	That will be all, Regina!

REGINA *flounces out.* FR MANNING *is looking at* MRS AYLWARD, *who turns away from him.*

OLIVER	Yes, I'm tired, very, very tired.

His mother and the priest watch as he walks out, slowly.

FR MANNING	I think something should be done with that girl. I don't like the way she behaves.
MRS AYLWARD	Poor, poor Oliver.
FR MANNING	Indeed. You can say that again. God Almighty, didn't you hear his talk! Well? Don't you have anything to say? Can't you say something?

MRS AYLWARD   It's odd. Living here on my own. Isolated. I've
               come to the very same conclusions as Oliver. It's
               as if he and I, instead of being separated, had
               been in constant contact over the past few years.
               But I've been afraid, so afraid, to open my
               mouth. Until my son said exactly what I felt. He
               spoke for me.

FR MANNING   Well, God help you. That's all I can say.

MRS AYLWARD   It's easy to call upon God.

FR MANNING   That's enough of that, now! I've put up with this
               for far too long. Very well. I've been a friend of
               the family for a long, long time. I've tried to help
               you with your business arrangements in the
               little way that I could. But I can be silent no
               longer.

MRS AYLWARD   (*Distracted*) I beg your pardon.

FR MANNING   Not as your friend, as your priest!

MRS AYLWARD   As my priest, what?

FR MANNING   You talked about the past a while ago.

MRS AYLWARD   The past?

FR MANNING   I have to remind you of the first year of your
               marriage.

MRS AYLWARD   I don't need reminding!

FR MANNING   Oh, but you do — you do. Scarcely a year gone
               and you nearly destroyed your life. Walked out
               bag and baggage. He begged you to go back.
               But no. You were determined.

MRS AYLWARD   (*Outburst*) Have you forgotten how I suffered
               with that man!

FR MANNING   (*Dismissive*) Suffer — happiness — unhappiness!

MRS AYLWARD   Yes, happiness! That's all that matters!

FR MANNING   Y'know, that's what's wrong with the world. All
               this craving for so-called happiness. What they
               really mean is self-indulgence. Yes. Oh, I know
               what I'm talking about. Oh, please, Helen, think
               of your salvation! You were a married woman,
               Helen —

MRS AYLWARD   You know very well what a monster he was —

FR MANNING   I only knew what was told to me about him.

MRS AYLWARD So now you don't believe what I told you?

FR MANNING I didn't say that. Anyway. You were married. You believed in your married vows. Didn't you? So it was your duty to live with them. But, no. You abandoned him just when you might have helped him. Irresponsible and irresponsible towards others into the bargain.

MRS AYLWARD Others? You mean yourself, don't you?

FR MANNING Yes. You shouldn't have come near me that night.

MRS AYLWARD Where else could I have gone?

FR MANNING If your marriage had become a cross you should have borne that cross!

MRS AYLWARD Just like that?

FR MANNING My God, Helen, have you any idea of the strength I had to find to send you back? (*Disturbed pause*) Anyway. At least you must admit it turned out as I said it would. Didn't it? Martin turned over a new leaf. Look at how responsible he became. And then there was the second great lapse in your life —

MRS AYLWARD The second what?

FR MANNING Oliver —

MRS AYLWARD I never failed Oliver!

FR MANNING You nearly wrecked your marriage and you're now allowing your son to wreck his life as well!

MRS AYLWARD No!

He goes into a kind of routine, the words rifling out.

FR MANNING You know the pact we had once? That we would tell one another, face to face, as honestly as we could —

MRS AYLWARD Yes.

FR MANNING Our weaknesses. Our failings. Didn't we? (*She nods*) So that we could try to better ourselves. (*She nods again*) Well, then.

MRS AYLWARD I know my weaknesses.

FR MANNING	Yes, but you wipe them out.
MRS AYLWARD	I don't. (*Pause*) Do I?
FR MANNING	All your life you've been headstrong and un-disciplined.
MRS AYLWARD	That is true, yes.
FR MANNING	Anything that came in your way you threw it off —
MRS AYLWARD	(*Whisper*) Freedom —
FR MANNING	But this isn't freedom. It's self-indulgence. When it didn't suit you, you walked out on your husband. When it didn't suit you to be a mother, you got rid of your son.
MRS AYLWARD	(*Cry*) I suffer for that —
FR MANNING	Look at the end result of it. Your son is now a stranger to you.
MRS AYLWARD	He's not a stranger to me! How dare you!
FR MANNING	You know that some terrible change has come over him.
MRS AYLWARD	I know no such thing!
FR MANNING	It's obviously difficult for you to accept it.
MRS AYLWARD	I worry about him. He is so idealistic. Don't you remember? How idealistic you were at that age? Ah, you've forgotten!
FR MANNING	I never forget anything.

She looks at him. Rises, moves away while he watches her.

MRS AYLWARD	Very well. I'm going to tell you everything. Do you realize that you cut yourself off from us? For years?
FR MANNING	Please, Helen. Don't!
MRS AYLWARD	Years. I wonder if you'd be in this house at all if it weren't for that new building out there.
FR MANNING	You have to understand my position —
MRS AYLWARD	Oh, yes. That hysterical woman. The runaway wife. You have to watch out with these danger-ous women.
FR MANNING	Oh, come on, now!

MRS AYLWARD	All these years. You never once came near me. You would hardly speak to me on the phone. And now here you are like some fire and brimstone sermonizer. You had better know the full truth about Mr Martin Aylward.
FR MANNING	What truth? What are you talking about?
MRS AYLWARD	He never reformed. From the day of our marriage to the day of his death he lived a life of brutal, sadistic self-indulgence —
FR MANNING	I don't believe it.
MRS AYLWARD	'The joy of life,' that's what you said earlier, wasn't it? You said he was 'full of the joy of life'. Hah! There was no joy in his sexual craving, only a kind of terrible desolation —
FR MANNING	How did you put up with it?
MRS AYLWARD	Duty, Father.
FR MANNING	Don't mock me, please.
MRS AYLWARD	It wasn't the promiscuity that was the worst, it was the emptiness.
FR MANNING	Can you make the distinction?
MRS AYLWARD	But the greatest sin of all was mine. The hypocrisy — What will people think? To conceal evil is the greatest evil of all. How I tried! Riddled with shame. And that man — charming and political in public. Don't you remember him? The photographs in the papers. Sometimes I wanted to shout out the truth. In the middle of High Mass, maybe. Or during a speech by one of our eminent TDs. But, no. In this country we are so good at concealment. And then came the final humiliation, the final act of shame.
FR MANNING	I don't think I want to hear any more.
MRS AYLWARD	You must! You're the one I must tell! It actually happened here, this very room. The maid was out there. Regina's mother. And I heard something. A kind of scuffle. Then her words, clearly. A mixture of fear and giggling. 'Let me alone, Mr Aylward,' she said. 'Let me alone.'

FR MANNING   Maybe it was a moment of — indiscretion.

MRS AYLWARD   My dear friend, my husband was Regina's father.

FR MANNING   And Jacko English! He's not her father, so? Does Oliver know this?

MRS AYLWARD   Oliver knows nothing. I swore to myself that no matter what was happening I was going to take over. I took charge of everything. That rotting hulk who was my husband said nothing. How could he? I had him under my thumb. I arranged the girl's affairs. I then made sure that Oliver would have some life, some freedom away from this house. I sent him away. It was like the death of a child to me. And I worked. That man was incapable of anything. He just sat there, sunken in a chair. Everyone said — isn't he wonderful! Isn't it marvellous the way he lets her run the business! When in truth I kept everything going —

FR MANNING   And that building out there? You've made it a memorial to him! What are you doing!

MRS AYLWARD   You would say it's my guilt, wouldn't you?

FR MANNING   Oh, stop!

MRS AYLWARD   Actually, I've always wanted to help battered women, women and their children. At least it started out that way. But I was well aware of the irony of what I was doing. Using his name like that.

FR MANNING   But everyone thinks it's his legacy. I'm not sure that I can go ahead with this. Not sure. Not sure, at all.

MRS AYLWARD   Rubbish. Of course, you can. My real reason for all this was that I was determined his money would be put to some good use. And, above all, I wanted to ensure that none of it would come to Oliver.

FR MANNING   And what will you live on?

MRS AYLWARD   What I've earned myself.

FR MANNING   And Oliver?

MRS AYLWARD   I've provided for Oliver.

FR MANNING And Regina?

MRS AYLWARD I will provide for Regina, too.

FR MANNING Just don't know how to put this — well — I think there may be some kind of — well — intimacy between the two of them. I've watched them.

MRS AYLWARD I know. There is.

FR MANNING You know!

MRS AYLWARD I know that nothing has happened between them, so far.

FR MANNING Good Lord! I should certainly hope not! Brother and sister! The very thought of it!

MRS AYLWARD Oliver was always given to passing phases. I'm sure he'll get over it. Besides, we'll have to find somewhere else for Regina.

FR MANNING Are you sure you haven't made a terrible mistake? About her birth?

MRS AYLWARD No mistake.

FR MANNING Are you sure?

MRS AYLWARD Of course I'm sure. Regina's mother, Joanna, told me the whole sordid story. I confronted Martin with it. He flustered and blustered, of course. In the end he owned up to it. I covered his tracks for him.

FR MANNING No, you couldn't have let that get out. He'd have been ruined at the time.

MRS AYLWARD Oh, I was the perfect wife! Yes. Smiling and nodding in public. Is it ever any other way for women?

FR MANNING How did you — you know — deal with Joanna?

MRS AYLWARD Plan was to ship her off to London. But she had other ideas herself. Whole thing — incredibly corrupt.

FR MANNING Well, you have to do things sometimes to avoid giving scandal to others. There's a higher motive —

MRS AYLWARD (*Spat out in anger*) Unutterably ugly and corrupt! She was paid. She said she'd go back to Jacko English whom she despised. And he was paid.

Everyone was paid. She told him some cock-and-bull story about an American and how she was paid off by the Yank. They got married, Jacko and she. Sure, you yourself married them! I nearly forgot that detail.

FR MANNING And that man had the nerve — when I think about it! Bare-faced. He stood in front of me and told me how he had got the girl into trouble —

MRS AYLWARD What else could he say? In these situations there's no space left for the truth.

FR MANNING After all the trust I put in him. Oh, Jacko English. Tch, tch, tch.

MRS AYLWARD It was no different to my marriage. I was bought off too, wasn't I? And my spouse was even more contaminated. Of course, there was more cash in my case —

FR MANNING Stop talking like this!

MRS AYLWARD Why? It's true, isn't it?

FR MANNING It's — perverse.

MRS AYLWARD Is it now? Is it any different? It's just one kind of barter is socially acceptable because there's a wedding ring, but the other isn't. Lives measured in lump sums.

FR MANNING You didn't marry Aylward for his money.

MRS AYLWARD Not consciously, no. I thought of it as — a good catch. Isn't that what they used to call it? When it really came down to the same thing, hard cash.

FR MANNING But your own feelings told you what to do.

MRS AYLWARD (*Sharp cry*) My own feelings told me no such thing!

They are both upset by this.

FR MANNING We should change the subject.

MRS AYLWARD (*Low*) No. You know how I felt about you at the time.

FR MANNING Please don't go on like this. I'm not sure I could cope. What's done is done.

MRS AYLWARD All I'd like to know is: what did you do with

your feelings? Did you put them into cold storage or something? I'd really like to know.

FR MANNING I can't answer questions like that. (*Dismissive*) Amateur analysis. I did whatever was necessary. I can always do whatever is necessary.

MRS AYLWARD It would help me to know. It really would. You see I can't just turn my feelings on and off like a tap.

FR MANNING 'Twould be far better for the two of us now if we just looked to the future.

MRS AYLWARD I wonder if people would turn out differently if they were to live with different people. You'd be different if you'd lived with me, I bet you would, now.

FR MANNING That's a comical notion and no mistake.

MRS AYLWARD It's as if you deliberately stopped some essential part of yourself from growing. What was so pure, so innocent, so good in a young man is something else entirely in a man of your age. Funny, isn't it?

FR MANNING You worry me when you're like this.

MRS AYLWARD All my life I was afraid to stand up in front of them and say, this is what I want out of life, this is what I *need*. Now it's too late. If I had any gumption I'd tell Oliver what his father was really like —

FR MANNING Don't do that, please!

MRS AYLWARD I'd tell him about Regina —

FR MANNING No!

MRS AYLWARD We've both denied life, you know that? Only difference is it's given you strength and left me a wreck.

FR MANNING Time. That's all. It's a matter of time healing. (*Pause*) Believe me I know how time heals.

MRS AYLWARD If I thought — but I wouldn't have the nerve — if it were to give him any happiness I'd say to them, Oliver and Regina, go ahead and give yourselves —

FR MANNING (*Deeply shocked*) You'd what!

MRS AYLWARD Yes, but I'm too much of a coward —

FR MANNING You're not a coward. You're a thoroughly disturbed woman.

MRS AYLWARD I'm frightened — of ghosts. Oh, I don't mean — Do you know what I think is really ghostly in this life? Things inside ourselves that haunt us, stopping us from being fully alive, being fully ourselves. Sometimes it's other people, sometimes it's what we've been taught. Our minds are haunted by dead, ghostly teaching. The future will find it all ridiculous. They'll say: how on earth could civilized people believe in such rubbish? And meanwhile the place is full of haunted, suffering people. Specially women. Oh, yes. Always women.

FR MANNING (*Cry*) Oh, God forgive me! Is that all I achieved for you out of the hardest battle of my whole life?

MRS AYLWARD I'm sorry.

FR MANNING I thought I had saved you.

MRS AYLWARD Maybe you did, but not in the way you wanted.

FR MANNING And I thought I had subdued my own weakness, my own frailty.

MRS AYLWARD You did something terrible to both of us.

FR MANNING Do you really believe that, Helen?

MRS AYLWARD I do. (*Long pause*) D'you know? Talking of Jacko English. I had him up here before you arrived. D'you know what he said? Tell Fr Manning, says he, to come and say a few prayers to bless the end of our work on the buildings. Oho, the bould Jacko!

FR MANNING Did Jacko really say that?

MRS AYLWARD Oh, and candles. He wants you to light candles as well.

FR MANNING Well, isn't that wonderful! That's Jacko, decent underneath it all. (*She begins to laugh*) Why're you laughing?

MRS AYLWARD You're a total innocent, a big schoolboy, that's what you are! I could take you in my arms this

	minute and give you a big hug.
FR MANNING	God bless us, such a thing to say.
MRS AYLWARD	Oh, don't be afraid. I'm not going to bite you! (*She touches him, lightly, on the arm, but he turns away*)
FR MANNING	(*Breaking away*) But Regina — Jacko's scheme — 'twould take care of Regina, wouldn't it? — The problem solved, maybe far away from here —

> REGINA *and* OLIVER *come quickly into the conservatory. She is carrying a tray of lunch things but they enter as if dancing. They have clearly been fooling about outside. The atmosphere is one of games, pranks, but with that suggestion of sexual attraction.*

REGINA	No, no, Mr Aylward. Don't! Leave me alone, now, Mr Aylward. Leave me alone.
FR MANNING	(*Turning, too*) What's that? What was that?
MRS AYLWARD	(*Shocked whisper*) Ghosts! Ghosts!

> *All freeze. Slow lights down.*

ACT TWO

Lights up. REGINA *and* OLIVER *are in the conservatory.* REGINA *is half-heartedly clearing up after lunch.*

OLIVER   (*Outburst*) But if you only knew! If you only knew how much I need you to be near me.

REGINA   First off you say nice things to me. Next minute and before I know it you're pushing me off. (*Heavy irony*) 'Course I'm only the maid —

OLIVER   No, no!

REGINA   — I dunno what to make of it.

OLIVER   I need your strength, Regina. Can't you understand that?

REGINA   What d'ya mean be that? Do you find me attractive, so?

OLIVER   It's like you have this simple, inner, perfect belief in yourself. Like something in nature. I feel there's nothing you wouldn't be prepared to do. Am I right?

REGINA   (*A rise in confidence*) D'ya think I could be painted? You know, you could paint a picture of me! I often think about that. Do you remember? You used to talk about, well, me skin.

OLIVER   I'm finished. I'll never paint again.

REGINA   The way you used always talk about us going away. 'Member? To Paris and places. I've been looking at pictures in books out of the library. Y'know? The way you told me to.

OLIVER   All the depth and texture — gone. Everything dead!

REGINA   Tha's what kept me going here all those years. I can stick it just by thinking of all the time we spent talking together. The things ya used to say.

36

	I say them over and over. When I'm on me own. At night.
OLIVER	If I could only tell you. But I can't.
REGINA	Tell me what? Is it another girl? I don't mind. I really don't.
OLIVER	It's nothing like that.
REGINA	Listen. I know everything'd be all right. I just do. I just know it. Besides, I'm not like one of those wans, y'know, who'd force you into anything.
OLIVER	What're you talking about?
REGINA	For us to go to bed together. (*Long pause*) OK. Forget it. I'm sorry I opened me big mouth.
OLIVER	It's not like that.
REGINA	That's OK. Just don't say another word, OK?
OLIVER	— but you don't understand.
REGINA	I understand I've made a right fool of meself. And all that talk you used to go on about. About people being free and all that stuff.
OLIVER	I still believe that.
REGINA	About you should be able to have sex if you wanted to.
OLIVER	That too —
REGINA	Doesn't sound like it to me. Maybe I'm not good enough for you?
OLIVER	I can't make love to anyone! Ever again!
REGINA	I see. Is it that you can't?
OLIVER	I'm not impotent, if that's what you mean.
REGINA	Maybe I'm not attractive enough for ya. Am I? Attractive, I mean? God, I shouldn't be talking like this, so I shouldn't.
OLIVER	It's that I'm — infected.
REGINA	Oh.
OLIVER	I hate my own guts.
REGINA	Don't say that. Whatever it is, don't say things like that. 'Tisn't right.
OLIVER	I'm just a walking corpse.
REGINA	Can't they do something for you? (*He shakes his head, unable to look at her*) I see. Aren't you alive, anyways?

OLIVER I'm going to die, Regina.

REGINA That's awful talk! Why're you talking this way? It's — creepy, that's what it is.

OLIVER I don't mind the pain. Oh, I do, but more than anything else it's that cold emptiness. Do you know I've begun to develop this incredible attachment to even stupid things. A few prints. An old palette knife. An old worn tweed jacket. I can't bear the thought of separation from everything in my room upstairs.

REGINA Such an ass I was. Me head in the clouds. There's something up with this house. I swear to God there is. I'm going to get out of here first chance I get.

OLIVER You're not listening to me, Regina! — Our closeness. It can't just end like this. We shared so much.

REGINA Like what?

OLIVER — our years together —

REGINA It's not that I've a big thing about sex. I don't. But it's what makes the world go round. Anyways. What's past's past.

OLIVER The one thing I dread is not having someone I can talk to. At the end. Mother, of course. But you're different, Regina. You were always so simple and clear about everything.

REGINA I have to think of meself so I have.

OLIVER But I can give you everything.

REGINA What everything?

OLIVER Everything I have. When I'm gone.

REGINA And what do I have to do, so? In return?

MRS AYLWARD *calls, off.*

MRS AYLWARD Regina! Regina!

REGINA *rushes away to avoid her.* MRS AYLWARD *enters the living-room and looks up at* OLIVER.

	Won't you come and sit with me, dear?
OLIVER	And where's his reverence?
MRS AYLWARD	Jacko English asked him down to the new building. To bless the work.
OLIVER	His holiness has gone to bless the lost souls of all the lost women of the world!
MRS AYLWARD	(*Outburst*) I wish you wouldn't smoke!
OLIVER	Sorry.
MRS AYLWARD	And I wish you wouldn't drink so much. Why am I nagging? Why am I going on like this?
OLIVER	I'm only trying to kill myself.
MRS AYLWARD	Oliver. Please!
OLIVER	'S true, actually.
MRS AYLWARD	What's wrong?
OLIVER	Where's Fr Manning?
MRS AYLWARD	(*Distraught*) I've just told you — what's the matter? There's something the matter ever since you walked in that front door. Oh, Oliver, dearest, I don't mean to pry. I don't. Don't think that —
OLIVER	I don't think that —
MRS AYLWARD	Questions, questions. Complaints, complaints. You must think me dreadful. It's no wonder I drive you away —
OLIVER	You're not like that.
MRS AYLWARD	(*Flustered*) Sometimes — maybe. Am I not? Really? Tell me that again.
OLIVER	(*Heavily*) You — are — not — like — that. I'm actually very glad to be home. I'm glad to be with my mother again. To be close to her.
MRS AYLWARD	Oh, my dearest!
OLIVER	Even though the country drives me nuts. And this bloody rain. Plus the fact that I'm finished.
MRS AYLWARD	What do you mean? Finished?
OLIVER	I'll never do anything again in my life.
MRS AYLWARD	Oh that's nonsense, utter nonsense!
OLIVER	(*Quietly*) Are you really glad I'm home?
MRS AYLWARD	What a question to ask! Of course I'm glad you're home.

OLIVER   Are you glad I want to be close to you?

MRS AYLWARD What are these questions? I don't deserve this
             kind of interrogation, Oliver.

OLIVER   No? There was a time when you dumped me.

MRS AYLWARD I never dumped you. There were good reasons
             why I had to have you out of this house.

OLIVER   Such as?

MRS AYLWARD Your father. We've gone over this time and time
             again, Oliver. Dumped! What an expression!

OLIVER   Have you any idea of the damage it did to me?

MRS AYLWARD Yes, I do. And of the damage it did to me, if
             that's any consolation to you.

             *Silence. He prowls up and down before her and she
             watches him, fearfully. He stops.*

OLIVER   I have to tell you something.

MRS AYLWARD (*She can hardly speak, as if she's been waiting for this
             for some time*) What is it?

OLIVER   I couldn't write it in a letter —

MRS AYLWARD For God's sake, Oliver, what is it?

OLIVER   It's not the end, OK? Remember that, no matter
             what I say, it's not the end of the world.

MRS AYLWARD You're sick!

OLIVER   I'm not sick. Not in the usual sense of the
             word —

MRS AYLWARD It's that terrible tiredness —

OLIVER   — yes —

MRS AYLWARD — not just flu?

OLIVER   No.

MRS AYLWARD Have you been to a doctor?

OLIVER   Yes. For God's sake, calm down, Mother. All it
             means at present is that I can't do my work.

MRS AYLWARD Is that all?

OLIVER   All! All? It's everything to me, my work. Every-
             thing!

MRS AYLWARD (*Deep breath*) Have you picked up something,
             Oliver? Is that it?

OLIVER   Yes.

MRS AYLWARD Well? Aren't you going to explain yourself?

OLIVER (*Breaking patience*) And now we're going to have the outraged mother. (*Sudden fury*) Is that it? Is that all you can say? Explain yourself! Oh, for Christ's sake! (*Sudden drop, eyes closed*) Sorry — sorry — sorry —

MRS AYLWARD (*Pause*) Is it syphilis?

OLIVER No, it's not. It's infinitely worse.

MRS AYLWARD Worse!

OLIVER They said to me, you have to tell her. Tell her simply, precisely, completely. After that, they said, everything depends upon love. Well. I've been diagnosed HIV Positive. I've already developed some of the classic symptoms of immune deficiency.

MRS AYLWARD Jesus, Mary and Joseph! That thing they're talking about in the papers?

OLIVER Now don't panic, Mother —

MRS AYLWARD (*Lost*) Don't panic, don't panic —

OLIVER — there are procedures to be followed — arrangements —

MRS AYLWARD (*Explosively*) That man! That bastard of a man!

OLIVER Who're you talking about?

MRS AYLWARD (*Wildly*) I curse the day I ever let him touch me, filthy, filthy hands! He has done this! Yes. I can see it. From beyond the grave, his foul touch, his own son —

OLIVER Rubbish, Mother — go and get a grip on yourself.

MRS AYLWARD The sins of the father are visited upon the children!

OLIVER It's not remotely like that. I'm shocked at you. I really am. That you'd believe such superstitious nonsense. That's not the way this infection passes. Don't you know that?

MRS AYLWARD (*Great definition*) I'm — not — talking — about — something — physical.

OLIVER Then what're you talking about?

MRS AYLWARD Character! Hasn't he infected you with his filthy

	habits? It's just the same as if he had infected you from beyond the grave. You're just like him!
OLIVER	I see. (*Long pause*) Yes. I am, amn't I? Just like him.
MRS AYLWARD	(*Whirling in a new direction*) Oh, my poor boy. We must get you a doctor, the very best there is, immediately, nothing will be spared. What is the prognosis? Have they told you? Who did you see? Can you believe them? There might have been a mistake, you know, in the tests — it happens. I read in the papers —
OLIVER	(*Pulls her up*) No mistake.
MRS AYLWARD	We have to put everything else aside now. Nothing else matters, now, nothing —
OLIVER	What'd you say about my father?
MRS AYLWARD	It doesn't matter.
OLIVER	— matters to me —
MRS AYLWARD	— forget about him —
OLIVER	No, I will not forget about him!
MRS AYLWARD	Oh my God, you are even beginning to look like him! Fr Manning was right!
OLIVER	(*Slowly, clearly*) I don't need a doctor, Mother, not now. I know exactly what has to be done. Or, rather, I know the choice facing me.
MRS AYLWARD	I'm just so broken, Oliver.
OLIVER	And I just need your help to make that choice. That's all. Just a question of accepting exactly what you know to be true — Then act on it!
MRS AYLWARD	(*Pain*) Oh — the truth! Don't give me truth!
OLIVER	You see, that's why I came home.
MRS AYLWARD	Oh, come here to me —

She embraces him. He breaks away.

OLIVER	Let's have a drink! Yeah! How 'bout some champagne?
MRS AYLWARD	Oliver! Really!
OLIVER	Sure. Why not? You always have champagne in the house, don't you?

MRS AYLWARD I don't think this is the moment.

OLIVER Of course it is! That's how you answer it, Mother. That's how you confront the big Boo-Boo. You laugh in its face. You let yourself go! If you're going to go down, you go down celebrating —

MRS AYLWARD Stop it! Stop it!

OLIVER Sorry. I'm not being flippant, you know. I mean it.

MRS AYLWARD That's what's so awful.

OLIVER Quite an event, isn't it? The opening of the Aylward Shelter for Lost Women or whatever it's called.

MRS AYLWARD Don't even mention that!

OLIVER Hah! The irony of it!

MRS AYLWARD I don't share your sense of humour.

OLIVER No, you don't, do you? How about that champagne?

MRS AYLWARD Oliver, you have to be patient with me. If it were only you and me, here — and this awful sickness — it would be all right. Don't know how, but it would be all right — but it's not just that. It's all my life as well and my life with that man — your father, long before you were born. It's as if it's all come together now, this very minute. I know you don't believe this but it's like being haunted by — ghosts —

OLIVER Don't believe in ghosts, I can only believe what's right in front of me.

MRS AYLWARD Yes, I know. I know that all too well.

OLIVER Don't think it matters a damn who we come from or who did what to us and when and where. We are each responsible for what we are. No one else.

REGINA *suddenly enters, from outside.*

I bet Regina would agree with me. Wouldn't you, Regina?

REGINA Oh, it's so dark in here. Let me put on the lights for yis.

MRS AYLWARD No!

OLIVER Oh, Mother, leave her alone. Go on, Regina, turn on the light. Turn on all the lights, Regina!

MRS AYLWARD sits, very distressed. REGINA, with some deliberation, does indeed turn on all the lights so that the scene is transformed.

You know? I haven't seen the sun once since I came home. Not once. Always the same grey, the same half-light. No sun, no sun —

REGINA Do you want anything else, missus?

MRS AYLWARD Yes. Get a bottle of champagne from the pantry. And a bucket of ice. And glasses. (REGINA *doesn't move*) Didn't you hear me?

REGINA Yes, missus.

She exits, unsure what's going on.

MRS AYLWARD I would do anything for you, Oliver.

OLIVER Anything?

MRS AYLWARD Anything. Why? Do you doubt me?

REGINA enters with a bottle of champagne and glasses.

REGINA There's no ice.

OLIVER So what!

REGINA exits again and OLIVER opens the bottle and pours two glasses.

MRS AYLWARD Just a little for me, please. I'm so very tired. You don't believe me, do you? That I would do anything for you?

OLIVER Fr Manning and yourself seemed very — pre-occupied at lunchtime.

MRS AYLWARD (*New idea*) Maybe you could talk to Fr Manning, Oliver?

OLIVER Are you joking! That creep!

MRS AYLWARD You don't know him!

OLIVER I don't want to know him!

MRS AYLWARD You only see the exterior. Behind that there's someone else, a frightened little boy perhaps —

OLIVER Oh, Mother, give me a break!

MRS AYLWARD — or maybe that's only what I want to believe. I don't know anymore —

OLIVER What do you think of Regina?

MRS AYLWARD What about her?

OLIVER Isn't she great? The way she's developed.

MRS AYLWARD Developed?

OLIVER (*Offering bottle*) Sure you don't want another drop?

She shakes her head, watching him as he drinks.

MRS AYLWARD Oliver. What are you thinking about? Just now?

OLIVER Well, I was just thinking. If I did have to be nursed or anything, Regina might — do it for me.

MRS AYLWARD Regina! That's outrageous, so it is!

OLIVER How is it outrageous?

MRS AYLWARD I'll nurse you myself if it comes to that. Regina!

OLIVER She understands me. I think she'd understand my needs.

MRS AYLWARD Oh, my God!

OLIVER She has this great vitality to be around.

MRS AYLWARD I won't hear another word of it.

REGINA *marches in with an ice-bucket.*

REGINA There's a few lumps of ice left in that.

They both watch as she marches back out again.

OLIVER Actually, I feel a bit guilty about her.

MRS AYLWARD Regina? Guilty? Precisely what are you going on about?

OLIVER   Well, I promised her a bit of a trip last year.

MRS AYLWARD   A bit of a what?

OLIVER   Oh, I was always telling her about Paris. About the shops and the style. You know the kind of thing. Then I discovered that she was reading about it.

MRS AYLWARD   Regina, reading? I don't believe it.

OLIVER   Oh, she had brochures. The lot. What was particularly impressive was that she had actually looked up the museums and art galleries. I thought that was pretty impressive. Don't you?

MRS AYLWARD   Maybe she knew who she was dealing with —

OLIVER   I'd forgotten all about it.

MRS AYLWARD   But she hadn't?

OLIVER   No.

MRS AYLWARD   (*Heavy irony*) Trust Regina! And now the two of you are off to Paris?

OLIVER   Don't make a joke of it, Mother.

MRS AYLWARD   What else is there to make of it? Paris, indeed!

OLIVER   What was so absolutely wonderful was to see her, well, almost grow, with the excitement of it. She looks so splendid, so full of the joy of life.

MRS AYLWARD   (*An intense whisper*) With the what? Do you realize what you're saying?

OLIVER   Just a moment — (*Calls*) Regina!

MRS AYLWARD   What d'you think you're doing?

OLIVER   — calling her in. Why not?

> *In a state,* MRS AYLWARD *turns away from him.*
> REGINA *appears, uncertainly, at the door.*

Go get another glass, Regina.

REGINA   But sure you have two already.

OLIVER   Get one for yourself.

REGINA   Mrs Aylward mightn't want me to, Mr Aylward.

MRS AYLWARD   Go get one, Regina.

> REGINA *departs. Mother and son are left in*
> *silence, looking at one another.* REGINA *comes*

back quickly with a glass in her hand. She looks
from one to the other.

(*To* REGINA) Oh, for heaven's sakes, sit down,
will you. (*To* OLIVER) Pour her some champagne.
Do you realize that you used a particular phrase
just now? The joy of life? What did you mean by
it?

OLIVER   Oh, y'know — everything I've ever painted that
was any way worthwhile was filled with a sense
of the joy of life, of the sheer delight in being
present, at this moment, in this life. There's
nothing else. That's our salvation. But it's so
easily threatened. That's why this place terrifies
me. I don't want to spend the bit of time that's
left to me in a place like this —

MRS AYLWARD   Even with me, Oliver?

OLIVER   You see, I'm scared, scared that everything I
believe in, everything beautiful and holy, would
be turned to dirt.

MRS AYLWARD   And you really believe that would happen here?
In your own home?

OLIVER   (*Vehemently*) Yes. Yes, I do.

MRS AYLWARD   And that's what Regina means to you?

OLIVER   Yes, I don't think she's like that. Are you, Regina?

REGINA   Maybe I should leave?

MRS AYLWARD   No, sit down. I'm now going to talk to both of
you. You must know everything. And then you
can both make your own choices.

The door opens on FR MANNING.

FR MANNING   God bless you all! We've had such a wonderful
time down there, Helen. You should have been
there. I truly believe it was a sacramental occasion.

OLIVER   And so was it here, too.

MRS AYLWARD   Come in, Father.

FR MANNING   First things first. Jacko will have to be helped to
set up his guest house and Regina is going to go

	and run it for him.
REGINA	'Deed I'll do no such thing!
FR MANNING	Oh, you're here, are you? And sitting brazen as brass with a glass in your hand! Tch, tch, tch —
OLIVER	I've plans for Regina, Father.
FR MANNING	What is this, Helen?
OLIVER	First off, a trip to Paris. On the other hand, if I'm stuck here I want Regina beside me, day and night.
REGINA	Beside ya?
FR MANNING	This is shocking, Mrs Aylward, truly shocking —
MRS AYLWARD	Nothing like that is going to happen, I promise you. Because for the first time I'm now free to tell the whole truth to these two.
OLIVER	What truth?
FR MANNING	Oh, Helen, you musn't, you mustn't!
OLIVER	I demand to know what the hell is going on!
REGINA	(*A cry*) Shush! Listen!

A pause. There is distant shouting. REGINA *walks into the conservatory and looks out.* OLIVER *joins her. Flames are reflected on them through the glass.*

	Will ya look! The new building's gone up in flames!
OLIVER	Quick! We have to save it! For my father's sake!

He and REGINA *both rush out.*

FR MANNING	But I've only just come up from there —

MRS AYLWARD *has gone to the door. She suddenly begins to laugh, a high, hysterical laugh which continues as she walks slowly out.*
   Lights down. Brief interval.

Lights up. Very early in the morning, shortly before dawn. The same room. Darkness outside with the glow of a great fire in the distance. MRS AYLWARD, *with* REGINA *to one side, standing, looking out. They are wearing their coats and scarves and look exhausted.*

MRS AYLWARD Everything gone up in smoke. The whole place. What a night. Where's Oliver?

REGINA He's still outside.

MRS AYLWARD Is he even wearing a coat?

REGINA No. Will I get him one?

MRS AYLWARD I'll get it myself. It's all burned anyway. Nothing left. Stay here.

REGINA Yes, missus. (*To the departing* MRS AYLWARD: *mimic*) I'll get it myself, so I will.

FR MANNING *rushes in through one of the other doors.*

FR MANNING Is she here?

REGINA She's just gone out this minute.

FR MANNING Oh my God, what's to become of us at all?

REGINA But how did it happen, Father?

FR MANNING Why are you asking me? What do I know about it? And that father of yours on top of everything else — I mean Jacko English. Insinuations! As if I hadn't enough to contend with. That blackguard!

JACKO (*Voice off*) Fr Manning! Are you there?

FR MANNING God Almighty, here he is again.

REGINA (*Shouting*) We're in here!

FR MANNING (*Gritted teeth, barely in control*) Shut up, will you.

Enter JACKO, *dragging his bad leg.*

JACKO So there ye are.

FR MANNING (*To* REGINA) Haven't you something to do, young one?

REGINA (*She's not going to move*) Mrs Aylward said for to stay put, Father.

JACKO Lord save us, but wasn't that a terrible night! Sure I thought sure and certain the whole place was for it, house and all. Isn't it strange the way things go now? What do you think, Father?

FR MANNING What, what, what?

He is walking distractedly here and there. JACKO *and* REGINA *watch him, then look at one another.*

REGINA *(To* JACKO*)* How'd it happen?

JACKO That'd be telling you. Wouldn't it, Father?

REGINA Why so?

JACKO Candles!

REGINA What candles?

JACKO Isn't that right, Father? *(Big whisper to* REGINA*)* We have him on the hop now, girl, I'm telling ya.

REGINA *(Excited)* Tell us!

JACKO Hould on there!

FR MANNING I must speak with Mrs Aylward at once —

JACKO Oh, I regret ever asking you to go down there in the first place, Father. To think the two of us might have caused it all —

FR MANNING Stop your babbling, English!

JACKO Lighting them candles caused it. I should never have involved you at all, Father, God forgive me —

FR MANNING That fire could have been caused by anything!

JACKO Oh, the candles, the candles —

FR MANNING I made sure that they were all out.

JACKO Whooosh! Just like that!

FR MANNING *(Rising hysteria)* I distinctly remember leaving that building secure.

JACKO *(Ignoring him, to* REGINA*)* Thing to do at all costs is to hush it up.

REGINA *(Going with him)* No one knows, barrin' ourselves.

JACKO If the papers were to get a hold of any of this, God Almighty, they'd make hay of it in next to no time. They do love digging up things about

	places like hospitals and schools and homes and that class a' thing.
REGINA	Sure no wan's going to tell them —
JACKO	Now ye're talkin', girl, ye're dead right. But sure I wouldn't open me mouth in a million years.
REGINA	I wouldn't breathe a word neither.
JACKO	Sure, we're all right so, then, aren't we, Father?

FR MANNING *is trying to decide what to say when a pale tense* MRS AYLWARD *enters, wrapped up against the cold.*

MRS AYLWARD	I can't get him to move. He doesn't listen to me. He is standing out there transfixed — Ashes! Ashes!
FR MANNING	Oh, thank God, you've come at last! We must speak —
MRS AYLWARD	Speak? You won't have to make a speech after all, Fr Manning.
FR MANNING	I was ready to make a speech —
MRS AYLWARD	About what? Charity for poor women? What a laugh. It's gone. And do you know something? It's an immense relief. It's as if something monstrous has been burned to the ground.
FR MANNING	You can't mean that?
MRS AYLWARD	Of course, I mean it. What time is it?
REGINA	'Tis nearly morning.
FR MANNING	But surely you want the fire investigated? To find out?
MRS AYLWARD	What is there to find out? There's nothing to find out. What are you doing there, Jacko?
JACKO	I'm waiting on the priest, missus.
FR MANNING	He's giving me a lift back to town. Would you prefer if I stayed?
MRS AYLWARD	Not at all. In fact I'd prefer if you went. I need to be alone with Oliver. And you must take everything with you. Documents, will, solicitor's file. Accounts. I'll sign over everything.

FR MANNING	But there's no need for this.
MRS AYLWARD	There is a need for me!
FR MANNING	But what about the interest?
MRS AYLWARD	Dispose of it! (*Pause*) And what will you do now, Jacko?
JACKO	Me? Oh, I'll be okey-dokey, missus.
FR MANNING	He and I need to have a long talk. Yes, yes. A good long talk. I don't like the way this man has been behaving, Mrs Aylward. I don't like it at all.
JACKO	I'm going to start a guest house, Mrs Aylward.
MRS AYLWARD	That'll be nice, Jacko.
JACKO	And Fr Manning's going to give me a leg-up. Aren't ya, Father? Just to get me started?
FR MANNING	You're a ruffian and no mistake, Jacko English.
JACKO	But, sure, you said I won't see you stuck. Them was your very words. And me fine daughter here is going to run it for me, aren't ya, Regina?
REGINA	Go 'n take a running jump for yourself!
JACKO	(*Threatening*) What'd ya say?

A shocked pause. OLIVER *has entered through the conservatory, gaunt, exhausted and wet.*

MRS AYLWARD	Oliver! My God, the cut of you!

She goes and embraces him, helping him to a seat.

JACKO	Answer me, miss!
REGINA	You can do what ya want. I'll even have a laugh watching you, but I never want anything to do with ya, ever again in me life, ever, and that's final!
FR MANNING	Come outside, Jacko —
JACKO	Did ya hear that, Father? Is that the way for a daughter to behave to her own father? Is it?
FR MANNING	Come on —
JACKO	Her own father! The little —

The priest has taken him by the arm, ushering him out, closing the door on him.

FR MANNING I'll be out to you in a minute!
OLIVER What's happening? What's going on?

> FR MANNING *gathers up his bag and papers, preparing to leave.*

FR MANNING Where's my bits and pieces? Time to say au revoir. Did you see my — anywhere — oh, there — Terrible night. Terrible night. At least no one was injured. I mean no one was — I suppose I'll be saying goodbye so, for the present. I'm not too far away at any time, if I can be of any — So much to be done. Not now, obviously. Time for cooler counsel. Well, that's it, isn't it? Pick up the pieces later. You are all in my prayers.

> *No one looks at him and he exits in silence.*

OLIVER It will all burn to the ground! There'll be nothing left of Father, anymore. I'm finished, Mother.
MRS AYLWARD No, dear. No, that's not true. (*To* REGINA) Fetch us a hot towel from the airing cupboard.
REGINA Is he all right?
MRS AYLWARD Just do as I say!

> REGINA *departs.*

That wasn't a good idea, Oliver, staying out like that. You're drenched.
OLIVER I am burning, Mother.
MRS AYLWARD Oh, Oliver, please don't —

> REGINA *comes back in with towels.* MRS AYLWARD *takes them and begins to dry his face and neck.*

Maybe you could sleep, Oliver? Would you like to sleep?
OLIVER I'm afraid to go to sleep.
REGINA Is he sick?

OLIVER   Close the doors.

MRS AYLWARD   What?

OLIVER   Close the curtains. Close the doors. Close everything. Do you hear me? I want everything closed. Turn on the lights.

MRS AYLWARD   (*Pause*) Do as he says, Regina.

A confused REGINA *begins to close doors and curtains, shutting out the conservatory.*

OLIVER   Is everything closed?

MRS AYLWARD   Yes, dear. Oh, Oliver, what can I do for you? Tell me!

OLIVER   Regina! Where's she gone to?

REGINA   I'm gone nowhere, Mr Aylward.

OLIVER   Come over here next to me. You'll stay next to me, won't you, Regina? When the time comes?

REGINA   He's talking like that again! What's wrong with him?

MRS AYLWARD   But I'm here as well, Oliver, can't I help you?

OLIVER   You can't help me like Regina can. Regina has the guts to do what has to be done. Regina knows about these things. Call me Oliver, Regina. Go on, call me Oliver!

REGINA   (*Pause, low*) Oliver —

OLIVER   You know what I'm talking about, don't you, Regina?

REGINA   You're upsetting Mrs Aylward, so you are! I don't think it's a bit right, so I don't.

OLIVER   You must stay with me to the very end.

REGINA   I think I should go, missus.

MRS AYLWARD   No. Sit down. I want to talk to both of you. Oliver? Are you listening to me? You must listen to me, Oliver!

OLIVER   (*Dully*) Yes.

MRS AYLWARD   It's about your father —

OLIVER   (*Suddenly alert*) What about him?

MRS AYLWARD   I lied to you about him and me. No, that's not true either. It's not black and white. Let's just say there's another version. Joy of life! What a strange phrase! It appears to be innocuous. Until you think about it.

OLIVER (*Wildly*) What about Father?

MRS AYLWARD What I said about him. The opposite may be true, may be truer. I'm able to see my own responsibility now, for the first time.

OLIVER For what?

MRS AYLWARD (*Almost lost in her own thoughts*) For that marriage. There's no one side to marriage, there are always two sides.

OLIVER I'm sorry, Mother. I know how much you've suffered.

MRS AYLWARD But how much did he suffer? It's only tonight, with all these insane happenings, that I've been able to ask myself that question. Oh, you should have seen him as a young man, Oliver! Full of vitality. Joy of life, indeed! Did I hate that energy all those years? I think I did, you know. Whereas, in fact, what I really hated was my own lack of moral courage in giving myself to a loveless marriage. The respectability! The horror of it all. Strange thing is that I became — stronger, in holding it all together down the years. What does that say about me, the kind of person I am?

OLIVER (*Whisper*) Please tell me about Father —

MRS AYLWARD (*Trying to gather herself*) Once upon a time — oh, once upon a time, Oliver, there was a little boy. He was brimming with life. But he was like an orphan. All around him was this withering denial of life. It was as if he should have been born in another place at another time. And as he grew up all his nature was turned inwards. There was nowhere for him to turn. So he lived two lives — the one they made him live in public and the one he was condemned to live in private.

OLIVER He was condemned!

MRS AYLWARD That's for sure — to live out a lie. Isn't that the ultimate hell on earth?

OLIVER Didn't you love him? Even a little?

MRS AYLWARD (*Pause*) No, I never loved him. You see, I lived out a lie, too. For all this! (*Ironic recognition*) All this!

OLIVER Don't you see what that says about me, Mother?

MRS AYLWARD I think I may have destroyed your life, Oliver. But isn't it something to recognize all this, even at this late stage? To try to gather the bits together. Make things — whole. It's not too late, is it?

OLIVER It's too late for everything, now.

MRS AYLWARD (*Lost in thought*) They taught me how to be a good wife. They taught me how a woman should keep her place. A woman has the greater role to play in life, they said. Did you ever hear such rubbish? A woman has to lead men in the path of virtue, they said. Oh, how well they know how to control women! Women are so easily tricked by appeals to their virtue. Make them feel good and they'll do anything. Not any more, Oliver, I've learned my lesson —

OLIVER Why didn't you say all this to me before?

MRS AYLWARD I was afraid.

OLIVER Afraid of what?

MRS AYLWARD Failure. What else? And then there's Regina here.

REGINA (*Jump*) What about me?

MRS AYLWARD You're part of this as well, Regina.

REGINA I don't know what you mean, missus.

MRS AYLWARD You and Oliver had the same father, Regina. Mr Aylward was your father, too.

REGINA (*Pause*) I see. And what about me mother?

OLIVER I don't believe this! I don't believe this!

MRS AYLWARD You'd better believe it!

REGINA So she was only a tramp, so —

MRS AYLWARD Your mother was a fine woman, Regina.

REGINA Explains a lot, don't it? At least I don't have to

	go near that clown Jacko English ever again. If you don't mind, Mrs Aylward, I'll be leaving now.
MRS AYLWARD	You're just upset. It's only natural.
REGINA	I'm going —
MRS AYLWARD	And where will you go?
REGINA	I have places.
MRS AYLWARD	I thought I could — help.
REGINA	Well, ya can't.
MRS AYLWARD	I haven't been very truthful to you, Regina.
REGINA	All your grand chat 'bout this and that and all ya wanted was to keep me a skivvy! Women this and women that. But what about me? Slaving and slobbering around this house morning noon and night for little more than the clothes on me back. Talk is cheap!
MRS AYLWARD	It's not just talk, Regina.
REGINA	— or maybe you kept quiet just to get your own back on him!
MRS AYLWARD	On who?
REGINA	Your man! Me — (*She is almost about to break*) That dead man!
MRS AYLWARD	That may be true, too.
OLIVER	Stop this! Both of you! I've got to — think.
REGINA	You never told me there was something up with him there, either. If I'd known there was something wrong with him it'd be different, I can tell you.
MRS AYLWARD	He's very ill, Regina.
REGINA	So I see. Such a fool I've been, with the wool pulled over me eyes. Know something? I thought there might be something between us. Him and me. I mean really between us. What a laugh! That's what it is, a laugh!
OLIVER	Regina, we can still be close —
REGINA	Not on your life. What do you take me for? I'm not a nurse or something. No way.
MRS AYLWARD	You may become too hard on yourself, Regina. I know.

OLIVER I can't believe this! What's happening?

REGINA Maybe Oliver there takes after his Da? Do you think, Mrs Aylward? And I take after me Ma? What would that make us, now? Wouldn't that make us into a family, do you think? By Christ, I'm not going to let this get to me! You were talking about the joy of life, weren't you? Well I have some of this joy of life in me, too, so I have.

MRS AYLWARD I'm sure you do.

REGINA Tell us something. Fr Manning. Does he know about all this?

MRS AYLWARD Yes. He does.

REGINA I see. Well, I'd better try and catch up with the two of them, him and Jacko, before they leave.

MRS AYLWARD What're you going to do?

REGINA First off, I'm going to latch onto Fr Manning.

MRS AYLWARD — latch onto Fr Manning!

REGINA Right! He's got all that money, now, hasn't he?

MRS AYLWARD But if it's only money, Regina, I can help you —

REGINA No thanks. I wouldn't touch it. I'm just as entitled to that money as that bastard Jacko English —

MRS AYLWARD 'Course you are.

REGINA The least you could have done was send me for training. Never mind. It's all water under the bridge. God, I can't wait to get out of here.

MRS AYLWARD You can always come back, Regina.

REGINA That's a laugh! Sure, the priest will look after me, won't he?

MRS AYLWARD It's all so — squalid!

REGINA Besides, if I'm really down on me uppers I can always take up English's offer in the B & B. He offered to set me up there, you know. Who knows who you'd meet there, says he. If you played your cards right now, Regina, you'd be rightly set up, so you would. Ho! He's a right pimp and no mistake.

MRS AYLWARD It can't be stopped —

REGINA So long, so.

REGINA *sweeps out.* MRS AYLWARD *moves as if to stop her physically but then sinks back. She looks at* OLIVER, *sunken in a stupor.*

OLIVER She's gone, isn't she?

MRS AYLWARD Yes.

OLIVER Whole thing's completely out of control and still somehow connected.

MRS AYLWARD Oliver, listen to me. Are you glad I told you about your father? I mean, does it make things more bearable?

OLIVER It doesn't make the slightest difference.

MRS AYLWARD But don't you even have any feeling for — what it was like for him!

OLIVER No.

MRS AYLWARD He was your own father!

OLIVER I didn't know my father. What are you talking about? Some kind of mystical connection? Come off it, Mother.

MRS AYLWARD It must mean something.

OLIVER Means bugger-all. Unless people are actually present, it means nothing. We are what we are. Regina was right. The only feelings that matter are the ones that are earned the hard way.

MRS AYLWARD Ghosts!

OLIVER The past is past. There is only the present. And the future. Or what's left of it.

MRS AYLWARD Don't you love me, Oliver?

OLIVER 'Course I do.

MRS AYLWARD You don't make it sound very convincing. What am I looking for?

OLIVER Anyway, these are just words. It's action that proves things. You've got to prove your feelings over and over again. No matter what the cost.

MRS AYLWARD Oh, I will prove myself, Oliver.

OLIVER Got to be able to accept everything —

MRS AYLWARD Oh, I do accept. I do, Oliver. You frighten me, Oliver, when you talk like this —

OLIVER What time is it now?

MRS AYLWARD	Must be nearly daylight. Have we really been at it all night?
OLIVER	Open a curtain!

She does so, opening the one into the conservatory. A faint light from outside.

MRS AYLWARD	Look! The light!
OLIVER	Regina would help me if she were here.
MRS AYLWARD	What's that dear? Oh, Oliver. It'll soon be a new day. Shall I tell you what I'm going to do for you? For us? I'm going to turn our house into a haven of peace and love. There will be just the two of us. Oh, of course, we'll get the very best medical attention that is. Of course, we will. But the important thing is to go on, to hope, to love, to care. You won't have to step outside that front door, Oliver. Everything you need will be here. And you'll be able to paint again —
OLIVER	Stop it, Mother! I'll never paint again.
MRS AYLWARD	This room is perfect for painting. It catches the sun whenever it comes out —
OLIVER	(*Near scream*) Stop it, stop it, stop it!
MRS AYLWARD	Don't want to upset you, Oliver, don't —
OLIVER	— need to arrange things —
MRS AYLWARD	Yes, of course, arrange things.
OLIVER	When the sun rises it will be perfectly clear, that perfect clarity. No dark corners. Nowhere to hide.
MRS AYLWARD	Hide? Hide from what?
OLIVER	It's worse than what you think. Much worse.
MRS AYLWARD	What is?
OLIVER	I'm riddled with it, Mother. I'm finished!
MRS AYLWARD	But you're fine. Perfectly fine. A bit run down, maybe.
OLIVER	For God's sake, Mother, I've just come through a massive glandular infection before I came here.
MRS AYLWARD	You never said that!
OLIVER	And now I'm beginning to break out.

MRS AYLWARD	For God's sake, Oliver stop talking like this. You're fine. You're fine.
OLIVER	I've begun to die. That's why you must help me.
MRS AYLWARD	(*Breathlessly*) But you walked about all evening — you went out — you helped with the fire — you talked to people. You did things! You can't be dying!
OLIVER	What do you think I was trying to do out there? I was trying to perish in the rain!
MRS AYLWARD	Please, Oliver, please don't go on like this. I can't stand it.
OLIVER	I deliberately stood in that rain as if it were raining death. I wanted it. I wanted it.
MRS AYLWARD	My poor boy, you're raving! You're not yourself.
OLIVER	We have to face it together, Mother. Exactly as it is.
MRS AYLWARD	I can't face it!
OLIVER	But you said you were strong enough to face anything — Please! For me!
MRS AYLWARD	Please, what?
OLIVER	I tell you, I'm not going to rot in that chair. I'm not going to wither away. There's life that isn't life at all. Will you be with me?
MRS AYLWARD	Of course I'm with you, Oliver, of course I am —
OLIVER	(*He produces a bottle of pills*) Look!
MRS AYLWARD	Oh my God, what's that?
OLIVER	I need to take an overdose.
MRS AYLWARD	Oh good God above — give me those, at once!
OLIVER	(*Sudden, childlike shiftiness*) No, because then you'd hide them on me.
MRS AYLWARD	Stop playing games, Oliver!
OLIVER	Regina would!
MRS AYLWARD	Are you out of your mind?
OLIVER	If I asked Regina she'd help me. She's strong!
MRS AYLWARD	No, she would not. Such a thing to say!
OLIVER	(*Working it out*) Regina knows when life's worth living. And when it's not. Regina would hold me. She'd help me swallow the pills. She would.
MRS AYLWARD	(*Loudly*) Regina would do no such thing!

OLIVER (*Challenging her*) Who are you?

MRS AYLWARD I'm your mother.

OLIVER Then you do it!

MRS AYLWARD (*Weeping*) But I'm your own mother, Oliver. I gave you life —

OLIVER Then take it back! I don't want to live anymore!

MRS AYLWARD I loved giving you life —

OLIVER Then love me by helping me to die!

She jumps up and begins to pull on a coat.

What're you doing? Where're you going? Don't leave me!

MRS AYLWARD Going for help. Can't stand this another minute. (*He grabs her arm*) Oliver — let me go!

OLIVER There must be no one else. Just the two of us. Please, Mother. Just the two of us. Don't humiliate me, Mother, not in front of others.

She holds him tightly and there is a long pause.

MRS AYLWARD That's better, isn't it? You mustn't frighten me like that, Oliver. I know how you like to frighten me. Everything will be just fine. You'll see. It'll be like old times, Oliver. You had such vitality as a little boy, Oliver, such liveliness. Look! The sunshine!

She throws open all the other curtains and dawn-light breaks into the room.

OLIVER (*Sunken back in the chair*) Is it the sun?

MRS AYLWARD What did you say, dear? Have you ever seen such a lovely morning!

OLIVER The sun — the sun —

MRS AYLWARD Oliver! Oliver! Don't sink down like that!

She pulls at him but he falls away, like a doll's head upon his shoulders.

Oh, God, what am I going to do? What am I going to do? That bottle! Where'd he put that bottle?

> *She wrestles with his clothing and finally stands, holding up the bottle of pills.*

OLIVER (*Still stupefied in the chair*) The sun — the sun —

> *The sunlight streams into the room as* MRS AYLWARD *looks down at* OLIVER *in the chair.*